Norbert Zimmermann

The Second Sinking of the TITANIC

"She was a beautiful ship. She looked stunning and that's how we should remember her."

Eva Hart, TITANIC survivor

Bibliographic information of the German National Library

The German National Library lists this publication in the German National Bibliography; detailed bibliographic data are available on the Internet at http://dnb.d-nb.de.

ISBN-13: 9783756257980

Production and publishing:
BoD - Books on Demand, Norderstedt

MIX
Papier aus verantwortungsvollen Quellen
Paper from responsible sources
FSC
www.fsc.org
FSC® C105338

Contents

Prologue

Since the first edition of this book was published in Germany, 8 years have passed since then, and a lot has happened regarding TITANIC research as well as the controversy surrounding artifacts recovered from the world-famous luxury liner. A controversy that has been smoldering since the official discovery of the wreck in 1985.

So, I decided to write a second, updated edition of my chapter entitled "The Second Sinking of the TITANIC" to bring my readers up to date. I paid special attention to updating the chapter " The Dispute about the Wreck of the Titanic as well, bringing it up to date.

I also decided to publish this book in English since it was previously available only in German.

I am very curious about the reactions to this book, and also curious because I am very critical of the salvage company, which has already been 're-flagged' so many times that it is difficult to keep track of who is in command.

After my first edition made its debut appearance in Germany it did not take long until the first of many disturbing fires were lit against me. I considered for a long time whether I should make it public, but at that time I had an online expenditure with the "Huffington Post" doing an advertisement for this book. No sooner had I published the article than the editorial staff of the

"Huffington Post" received an anonymous call denigrating me and my book in the worst possible ways. The negative talk went so far that my article was taken offline. Only after I called the editorial office and had a long conversation with the editor-in-chief was the article republished. It seems that I had struck a nerve in some folks with this book and I was to be silenced!

The reason for this backlash was, largely, due to my inclusion of the 'open letter from Paul-Henri Nargeolet to Dr. Robert Ballard', which is thematized by me in this version of the book. I had to learn, much to my horror, that this 'open letter' is not well known anymore even in 'expert' circles within much of the Titanic Community. It was largely due to this revelation that I was moved to write this new edition of my book. I have kept some chapters as they were written by me in the original version of 2014, while I have taken into account the latest developments in other chapters. I hope that this updated book will again captivate my readers and make them think.

Norbert Zimmermann

Introduction

The story of the TITANIC has been occupying people's minds for over 100 years now and has never left many of them.

The tragic sinking of the luxury liner on a moonless night on 15th April 1912 has lost none of its sad fascination to this day. More than 1,500 people lost their lives on that terrible night, and as was known then as it is today: it was absolutely avoidable!

After the tragedy, the wreck of the luxury liner disappeared from sight for over 73 years. It lies at a depth of 3800 meters and the technology to penetrate to such a depth was not available for a long time. Only since the wreck was discovered has it been possible to really answer some questions about how the sinking happened.

The expeditions to the wreck brought to light some very important findings, such as the breaking apart of the ship during the sinking and some more. But it also became clear very quickly that there was still a lot of money to be made with the TITANIC and this is where the "Second Sinking of the TITANIC" begins.

Many of the salvaged artifacts and memorabilia, such as personal letters of the passengers, were sold in auctions to the highest bidders. In this way, many wonderful things from aboard the TITANIC passed into private ownership without humanity having the opportunity to share in them.

Such things belong in museums and not in private hands!

A particularly sad case in point is the discovery of the perfume samples of the German-born passenger Adolphe Saalfeld. In his cabin he had left a leather case with 65 essence oils in small glass tubes, which he needed for his new perfume collection. Many decades later, these glass tubes were recovered from the seabed by the salvage company of the TITANIC and reissued as a new perfume, without, however, giving the descendants of Adolphe Saalfeld a single cent of the proceeds of the perfume.

So much for the promise once made by the salvage company to return all artifacts that can be clearly identified with a person to the relatives...

This book describes how the "Second Sinking of the TITANIC" took place and is still going on.

For all those who care about the history of the TITANIC, one can only hope that the wrangling over the wreck and her salvage rights will eventually come to an end and that there will be a reasonable solution to the problem.

But alone, I do not believe so!

The Posse around Robert Ballard, or Who Found the Wreck?

So much has been reported and written about the sinking of the TITANIC in the 100 years since her tragic end in the icy North Atlantic. So much has been reported and written about the sinking of the TITANIC that the impression has been created that everything on this subject has already been said. But this is not the case...

For example, the so-called "Discovery of the wreck of the TITANIC" by Robert Ballard and Jean Louis Michel, whose participation in the expedition is often dropped under the table; most laymen only know the name Ballard. Nobody really knows Michel, who had the same share in the "discovery" of the wreck (this is very controversial in TITANIC circles).

In historiography, Sunday, 1st September 1985 is the day on which Dr. Robert Ballard (and Jean Louis Michel) discovered the wreck of the TITANIC at a depth of 3800 meters. Since then, Ballard has been celebrated as the "Discoverer of the wreck of the TITANIC."

Side note: Even the video footage of the "discovery" of the TITANIC is not real. Since Robert Ballard was asleep in his cabin when the wreck was "found," it was

11

decided without further ado to recreate the discovery of the TITANIC wreck for posterity, this time with Robert Ballard. So, the famous chants of the crew of the research ship: *"A boiler, this is a boiler!"* with a celebrating Robert Ballard are just an illusion for posterity. So much for authenticity...

But were they really the first to find the wreck of the TITANIC back then?

There was a major earthquake in the TITANIC world in 2005 when Paul-Henri Nargeolet, who was co-leader of five expeditions to the wreck of the TITANIC, dropped the bombshell in an open letter to Ballard:

The wreck of the TITANIC was not discovered by Ballard, but eight years earlier by the British Navy!

HMS Hecate, a hydrographic ship of the British Royal Navy, was mapping the "paths of nuclear submarines" in the North Atlantic and discovered a "large shipwreck in two parts."

The big problem with the finding of the wreck of the TITANIC by HMS Hecate, however, is that it was supposed to have been a top-secret mission, and therefore, it was not allowed to become known that the British were in the area at all. So, the discovery of the wreck probably remained "top secret"!

To make one thing clear: Of course, Ballard and Michel tracked down the TITANIC on Sunday, 1 September 1985, and were the first to take pictures of the wreck for posterity, but whether they were really

the first to find the wreck, or parts of the wreck, is still
very controversial.

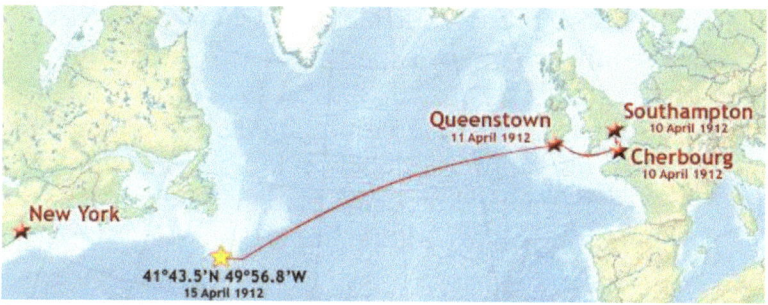

Source: public domain/Wikimedia commons

But why is it that since 1985, it has been firmly asserted
that Robert Ballard "found" the wreck and any attempt
to claim otherwise is almost treated as blasphemy?

The truth is as simple as it is banal: There is a lot of
money at stake in this matter, because if the truth about
some aspects of the wreck finding were to become
public, many would have to dress very warmly.

And what happens when someone swims against the
tide, a certain Jack Grimm had to experience first-hand.

For a better understanding: In 1981, during the second
of his three expeditions financed by himself to search
for the wreck of the TITANIC, the eccentric Texan oil
millionaire Jack Grimm (also called Cadillac Jack by
his friends) found a propeller blade of the luxury liner
that broke off when the ship collided with the iceberg.
But to this day, it is strictly denied that he really found
it...

13

The TITANIC historian Andreas Pfeffer has primarily examined the testimony of the Second Officer Charles Herbert Lightoller before the British Board of Inquiry and has come to a remarkable conclusion that has been consistently ignored by experts:

According to Charles Herbert Lightoller's testimony, the TITANIC lost a propeller blade in the collision with the iceberg, and this said propeller blade was found by Jack Grimm during his expedition in 1981!

Before the committee, Lightoller responded to Chairman Lord Mersey's question on 20th May 1912, as to whether he had felt the collision of the ship with the iceberg:

"It is best described as a jar and a grinding sound. There was a slight jar followed by this grinding sound. It struck me we had struck something, and then thinking it over, it was a feeling as if she may have hit something with her propellers. And on second thought, I thought perhaps she had struck some obstruction with her propeller and stripped the blades off. There was a slight jar followed by the grinding - a slight bumping."

Lord Mersey reeled in astonishment here and asked him:

"I understand you to say you thought it was the propellers?"

Lightoller's answer to this question was short and concise, but unequivocal: *"Yes."*

When Lord Mersey asked Lightoller if he knew where this noise came from, he replied:

"No, my Lord. Naturally I thought it was from forward."

"But you suspected the ship was losing a propeller blade? What did you do after you heard the noise?" Mersey continued.

"I went to see what was going on."

As the questioning continued, Officer Lightoller then became more specific. He stated that he overheard a conversation between the captain and one of the officers about the lost blade.

Lord Mersey then asked which propeller Lightoller thought had been affected.

"The starboard propeller, sir."

Mersey followed up and asked how Lightoller had noticed it. Lightoller replied to the presiding judge that the ship had subsequently "run out of round."

"Do you have any experience in this? I mean, has this ever happened to you so far in your career?"

"Yes sir. I have experienced this twice in my career on other ships, so I know how it feels. The propeller then runs out of round."

This is remarkable because a propeller blade is missing from the wreck of the TITANIC. As more and more questions arose as to why a propeller blade seemed to have gone missing there, more and more different explanations were given by the salvage company RMS Titanic Inc.

First, it was completely denied that the propeller blade was missing. It was claimed that it was buried in the mud and was therefore no longer visible.

In 1991, another expedition to the wreck of the TITANIC took place for the IMAX film "TITANICA." In this phenomenal film with breathtakingly clear shots, the propellers at the stern of the ship were seen for the first time. And look: It was clearly visible that a propeller blade was missing on the starboard side...

What to do now? The salvage company then claimed that this propeller blade broke off at the moment when the stern hit the seabed with full force before it finally came to rest.

However, this "explanation" is not valid insofar as the blades on the port side hit the seabed in the same way. But there, of course, no propeller blade is missing...

You can twist and turn it however you want, but one thing seems to be quite certain: The TITANIC lost a propeller blade in the collision with the iceberg!

The latest version of the story is that Jack Grimm found a propeller blade, but it was too small to be from the TITANIC. It's really interesting what else is claimed to cover up the truth...

All this charade just to avoid confirming that Jack Grimm found the propeller blade?

16

It looks like it, because in case this became fact, Grimm would have been the rightful discoverer of the TITANIC since he found parts of the ship, and RMS Titanic, Inc., would have no rights to the wreck of the TITANIC. If you then take a look at the original video footage of Grimm's expedition, you can't help thinking that he actually found the propeller blade. A "washed rock," as it is repeatedly claimed, does not seem to be visible there. Rather, it is indeed a propeller blade!

Regarding the discovery of HMS Hecate, some "experts" have developed their own view of things, claiming that HMS Hecate found a wreck, but that it was "a joke of the crew" that this wreck was the TITANIC.

Aha, a joke of the crew? So loosely based on the motto: *Ah look! A shipwreck! It must be the TITANIC, ha-ha-ha!"*

All you can really say to this is: Oh, my goodness. How stupid do they think people are? The worst thing about it is that many people in the so-called TITANIC community adopt these explanations one-to-one and don't even begin to question them.

Curiosity as a sidenote: More and more "former crew members" of HMS Hecate are now appearing, either shifting the year of discovery forwards or backwards, or denying altogether that the TITANIC was found. With the large number of "crew members", one inevitably wonders whether they were really on-board HMS Hecate or whether they just want to make themselves important.

Both the story of Jack Grimm and the story of HMS Hecate have one thing in common:

The nature of the story's almost bizarre denials!

For comparison

Jack Grimm:

- It was only "a washed rock" that Jack Grimm found.

- The TITANIC is not missing a propeller blade at all (only when it could no longer be denied was a missing propeller blade admitted).

- There is a propeller blade after all, but it is too small to have come from the TITANIC.

HMS Hecate:

- It was another shipwreck that was found, and it just happened to be broken in two like the TITANIC. This makes you involuntarily wonder: How many other large shipwrecks that are broken in two are still down there in relative proximity to each other?

- It was a "joke" of the crew that the wreck found was the TITANIC. (My absolute favorite...)

18

- The area of the discovery is wrong. after all, the TITANIC sank 13.2 miles west of the stated SOS position. However, the fact that it was never claimed that the HMS Hecate found the ominous "large shipwreck in two parts" exactly at the SOS position of the TITANIC is once again forgotten. That wouldn't fit in with the story...

- The HMS Hecate could not have found the TITANIC, otherwise the British would have confirmed it. But the "experts" seem to forget that it was a secret mission of HMS Hecate. And therefore, a "confirmation" was not possible, if the story about HMS Hecate is really true of course.

- Since the discovery took place in 1977, it could not have been known at that time that the TITANIC had broken in two, because that has only been known since 1985! And therefore, it was not the TITANIC that was found by HMS Hecate (what a strange logic).

- It was rocks that were thought to be a wreck. Interesting. What rock formations are supposed to look like a large shipwreck in two pieces? Also, again, this sounds suspiciously like Jack Grimm and his "washed rock"!

One then really wonders what kind of rocks these are supposed to be that look like propeller blades of a ship or even like a large shipwreck in two parts. And all this in a search area where the TITANIC was finally found.

It is quite striking that some experts (or those who think they are) carry the 13.2 miles distance to the stated position of the TITANIC in front of them like a mantra and think that they have found the killer argument for any discussion...

By the way: Jack Grimm found the propeller blade, according to his own statement, "between the indicated position of the sent SOS and the found lifeboats," so the 13.2 miles do not apply here. Bad luck!

All in all, it remains to be said that all these reasons sound like lame excuses just to preserve Robert Ballard as the "true discoverer" of the TITANIC. Only why would a Paul-Henri Nargeolet name HMS Hecate as the true discoverer of the TITANIC if it did not correspond to the facts? There had been these rumors about the Hecate for some time, but Nargeolet then confirmed them with his statement.

But I guess some "experts" have a suitable answer to that too... again.

Jack Grimm, by the way, would have nothing more to gain from being recognized as the discoverer of the TITANIC, or at least wreckage from her, as he died in 1998 at the age of 72.

Another, almost comical anecdote told by Andreas Pfeffer is the story about the so-called "compression fold" of the TITANIC. On the starboard side, near the front holds of the ship, there is a huge hole that is pressed outwards from the inside. This hole could not be explained at first, because it was much too high to have come from the collision with the iceberg. When the term, "explosion hole," was mentioned by some, the salvage company explained that it was simply a "compression fold" that was created when the bow of the ship rammed into the seabed.

So far, so good. But when the discussions about an "explosion hole" did not end, the salvage company came up with the bizarre explanation that the TITANIC was in a NATO exercise area and that they had registered its target coordinates for various orientation attempts. Therefore, it was quite possible that a torpedo had strayed and escaped there again. But how it can be explained that there is only one hole is not clear to the author. If there is an entry point, there must also be an exit point, right?

Therefore, the original explanation with the "compression fold" seems to be the more logical variant to me. The explanation is very plausible and certainly corresponds to the facts. But then why did the salvage company give this completely abstruse explanation with the torpedo? Nobody really understands that...

c) Sammlung N.Z.

On this model you can see the "compression fold" very well ©
authors collection

The "rights" of RMS Titanic, Inc., to the wreck of the
sunken luxury liner are very questionable anyway. It is
very unusual for an American court to presume to
award the rights for a shipwreck to an American
company that sank in international waters.

The TITANIC really is a special case, because a wreck
actually belongs to whoever finds it legally and can
salvage it in whole or in part. The TITANIC lies on a
submarine headland that belongs to Canada, but the
Canadians immediately announced loudly and in
writing that they had no interest in the wreck. Thus, it
would lie within international waters, which would

therefore enable anyone, if they had the wherewithal, to dive there and organize salvage trips.

Insurance-wise, the Cunard Line took over the White Star Line with "all rights and obligations" and owned the actual rights to the wreck, at least until 2012, when the one-hundred-year insurance contract expired. However, the Cunard Line also knows that the Americans have made the greatest efforts in the matter of TITANIC. It is therefore clear that they indirectly support precisely those salvage teams in order to keep other diving-minded businessmen away.

If one were to be precise, it would probably be enough if business-minded people were at hand, who would then simply dive to the wreck and bring salvage with them, then suddenly, according to salvage law, they would have the same rights to the wreck of the TITANIC...

Anecdote on the side: The Englishman Douglas John Faulkner Woolley has also been claiming the wreck of the TITANIC for many years! In 1966, Woolley had proposed to surround the hull of the TITANIC with hundreds of water-filled plastic containers and to run electricity through the containers. This was to release gases that would bring the huge ship to the surface.

Another of Woolley's proposals was to lift the TITANIC using air-filled nylon balloons. The whole project was supposed to cost 5 million dollars but failed. In the 1970s, Woolley founded the Titanic Salvage Company and staked his claim to the wreck. He sat down at his typewriter one evening and wrote himself a declaration of ownership for the TITANIC and sent it all over the world, to shipping companies (including the Cunard Line) and various courts and then waited for the appropriate deadlines. Since no objections were received from the authorities, Woolley considered himself to be in possession of the TITANIC wreck. He caused a great stir with his announcement that he wanted to find the TITANIC, lift her and tow her to Liverpool, where she would become a floating museum.

Over the decades, he tried to get experts and, above all, money to realize his plans, but he did not manage to raise the two million pounds he would have needed to be able to start at all. To this day, Douglas Woolley has never been to the site of the accident.

However, his latest "coup" is to lift the wreck of the Queen Elisabeth I, which burnt out in Hong Kong harbor in the 1970s. Unfortunately, Woolley simply cannot understand that the wreck of the Queen Elisabeth I was already scrapped at the end of 1975 and that individual parts of the ship were used, among other things, as building material for the construction of Hong Kong airport.

(C) Privatfotos Norbert Zimmermann

From left to right: Douglas Woolley, Norbert Zimmermann, and Gary Smith (Project Controller (Seawise Salvors International) (©Private Images Norbert Zimmermann)

Let's return to Jack Grimm and his propeller blade for a moment:

Until today, Jack Grimm is only portrayed as an eccentric weirdo who claimed that he had found a propeller blade of the TITANIC just so that he "had something to show at all"...

Since the coordinates of the propeller blade were known, Ballard had an easier time "finding the TITANIC" in 1985. Maybe he also knew the data of HMS Hecate and was of great help, who knows...

At least, Jack Grimm later claimed that it had provided Robert Ballard with all of its findings prior to the latter's 1985 expedition. However, Ballard strongly denies this. It would also not fit the heroic story Ballard has been telling for several years, that he first found two sunken submarines in a secret mission for the U.S. Navy and then also got a free hand to find the TITANIC.

But more about this in the chapter "The Open Letter from Paul-Henri Nargeolet to Robert Ballard"...

Scientific Evidence of the Sinking

The most important question that has arisen since 15th April 1912 is undoubtedly: How and, above all, why did the legendary TITANIC sink?

Two investigation committees tried to get to the bottom of this question, and based on the testimonies of the survivors, came to the conclusion that the iceberg had torn the TITANIC open like a sardine can over a length of almost 90 meters and that this had led to her sinking.

It was only when the wreck was officially found that some questions were clarified, while in turn new questions arose. The wreck of the TITANIC lies broken in two pieces at a depth of 3800 meters on the seabed. This was remarkable because until then, it was assumed that the TITANIC had started her journey to the bottom of the sea in one piece.

Now, after more than 35 years and many expeditions to the wreck of the luxury liner, the fog surrounding the events of that night has at least lifted somewhat.

The iceberg had not inflicted a gaping 90-meter-long wound on the ship´s hull, but rather several small damages in too many different parts of the vessel that led to the sinking of the TITANIC.

The theory surrounding the sinking of the ship was given a new twist in August 2005 when a group of scientists, divers and cameramen on board the Russian research vessel Keldysh set off for the wreck of the TITANIC.

For what the researchers found was a minor sensation. They discovered two previously undiscovered, complete bottom segments from the hull of the wreck. After months of investigation, however, the researchers only realized the full significance of this find, which led them to the conclusion that the last minutes before the sinking probably happened in a completely different way than previously assumed.

Based on the video images of the dive, exact drawings of the two pieces of the floor were first made. The pieces belonged together and formed an almost 21-meter-long element of the double bottom.

They come from the exact spot where the TITANIC broke apart. Until now, it was believed that the affected parts had broken into countless small pieces and were lost forever.

The wreckage then revealed what forces acted on the TITANIC at the critical moment.

The classic theory of TITANIC research was that the ship broke apart completely only a short time before it sank.

The stern rose more than 30 degrees, then the pressure became too great, and the construction tore apart from top to bottom, a scenario in which the passengers knew what was awaiting them.

The new find suggests it was different. The rupture probably began at a more acute angle., perhaps at less than eleven degrees, and then occurred in two steps.

Der Untergang der Titanic from Willy Stöwer © public domain

First, the superstructure of the TITANIC failed. The crack extended to the double bottom that was still holding the ship together. Thousands of tons of water suddenly pouring in finally pulled the hull down in the middle.

The upper decks pressed against each other, the bow sank and finally pulled the stern down as well. Only now did the connection between the bow and the stern break.

Expedition member Roger Long commented: *"It looked like the TITANIC would continue to sink very slowly and float for quite some time."*

But once the middle section of the TITANIC was filled up, everything happened very quickly. For the people on board, the end may have come as a complete surprise.

One phenomenon of the sinking that has been much discussed for years is undoubtedly that a large number of the survivors reported that the TITANIC sank in one piece.

There is a very simple explanation for this:

The people couldn't see the breaking apart of the TITANIC because it happened below the waterline - outside the field of vision of the survivors. In addition, the ship's lights were still on until a few seconds before the ship broke apart, then they turned off abruptly and it was pitch black. And there was no moon. The people in the boats could hardly have seen anything. Thus, some survivors only testified before the American investigating committee that they "had the feeling that the TITANIC broke in two," but not that they actually "saw" it with their own eyes.

Another new finding is that rivets were used in the construction of the ship whose durability was not high enough to withstand the collision with the iceberg.

Some of the rivets had been applied by machine, others by hand. A huge machine was used by the workers at the Harland & Wolff shipyard in Belfast to rivet the ship's skin. However, as this machine was too large to be used on the front part of the ship, this part was worked on manually.

Wrought iron rivets were used because they were easier to work with manually, but wrought iron is less resilient than steel. The workers were aware of this problem. To compensate for this weakness, a slag substance was added to the molten iron. By forming tiny glass particles inside the metal, the rivets could be made more durable. But the mixture of iron and slag is questionable. If the dosage is not correct, the opposite effect - namely the weakening of the rivets - can be the result!

In the case of the TITANIC, exactly this effect seems to have occurred, because the riveting of the ship shows clear weaknesses. Unfortunately, the concentration of the slag was such that it led to the weakening of the rivets.

When the ship then rammed the iceberg, the ship's side was dented, the rivets gave way, and the ice-cold seawater penetrated through the open seams into five compartments of the ship, condemning the TITANIC to sinking.

In the documentary "TITANIC - The Final Words," which was released in early 2012, James Cameron presented another very interesting discovery made during a new expedition to the wreck: A box containing the rockets of the TITANIC was found in the wreckage.

Until now, it was assumed that the crew of the sinking luxury liner only fired white rockets to draw attention to its plight that night. The discovery, however, presented a completely different picture: The box contained rockets in blue, green, red and white.

TITANIC historian Don Lynch had this to say about it: *"They were firing rockets with colored balls. They rose, and white and colored balls burst forth!"*

This ends almost a hundred years of discussion about what color the rockets were that were fired by the crew that night: They were colorful!

Another very interesting theory about the night of the TITANIC disaster was put forward by TITANIC historian Tim Maltin. According to his investigation, a special optical phenomenon occurred on the night of the accident: A so-called super-refraction!

Due to the thermal inversion, a layer of air cooled by the cold Labrador Current lay below a layer of air warmed by the warm Gulf Stream. Due to this effect, light was reflected unusually strongly, and a false second horizon was formed above the real one.

A haze formed in between, which the two sailors Lee and Fleet also noticed in the crow's nest. The calm sea also blurred the area between the two horizons so that the iceberg "disappeared" below the false horizon the sailors were looking at. Therefore, the iceberg was not spotted by Fleet and Lee until it was already too late.

Due to the super-refraction, distant objects also appeared closer - the reason why the crew of the Californian only perceived the TITANIC as a rather small and nearby ship. The (as we now know, colorful) signal rockets fired from there, therefore appeared to the crew to be too small with regard to the supposedly small size of the ship so that they were not perceived as important enough. Another problem was that the emitted Morse signals probably could not penetrate through the layers of air to the TITANIC.

This new theory shows clearly that the story of the TITANIC is still not over, even more than a hundred years after her tragic sinking!

How Much is the Wreck Really Damaged?

Since the wreck was found at a depth of 3800 meters, there has basically been an argument about how long it will take for it to fall into final decay. Of course, after more than 100 years at the bottom of the sea, it is clear the legendary shipwreck will not have too much time left, but it is absolutely unclear when that time will come.

After the discovery of the wreck, the salvage company claimed that the wood of the TITANIC had almost completely disappeared and that it was not known how this would affect the steel construction of the ship, which was still very good. Therefore, artifacts of the ship had to be salvaged "as quickly as possible," as there was not "much time left."

The only bad luck for the salvage company was that filmmaker James Cameron not only dived to the wreck for his blockbuster "TITANIC," but also for two other documentaries in 2001 and 2005. The myth of TITANIC had not left him either.

During his numerous dives, Cameron penetrated as far into the interior of the ship as no one had ever done before. He found out that large parts of the wooden interior were still completely intact.

What now? The salvage company has always been very resourceful. It was then quickly announced that the steel of the ship was "So bad and soft like chocolate." For years, the opposite was said, but what do I care about yesterday's talk? (By the way, this is a very common phenomenon by the company.)

A few small details in between: The salvage company at the time forbade James Cameron to use some of his interior shots of the wreck taken in 1995 in his movie. The reason for this ban seems to be that Cameron's interior shots showed too clearly that the wreck of the TITANIC was not in such bad condition as the salvage company claimed at the time. This, of course, ran completely counter to the salvage company's efforts to use the poor condition of the wreck as a hook for even more salvage operations. It was only in the course of his documentary film, "Ghosts of the Abyss," which was released in 2003, that the interior shots taken in 1995 resurfaced. Incidentally, it was also rumored that Cameron, after it became clear that he was not allowed to use the interior shots, went to Woods Hole to present his recordings to the astonished Robert Ballard...

Already in 1985, the US Congress had drafted a resolution that was passed as the "RMS Titanic International Maritime Memorial Act" under the registration number Section 450RR-450RR-6.

There it is stated:

A) <u>Findings:</u>

36

The Congress finds that

1. The RMS Titanic, the liner that sank on her maiden voyage after colliding with an iceberg on 14 April 1912, should be declared an international maritime memorial to the men, women and children who lost their lives on her;

2. The recent discovery of the RMS Titanic more than 12,000 feet (3658 meters) below sea level demonstrates the practical utility of oceanography and engineering;

3. The RMS Titanic, well preserved in the cold, oxygen-poor waters of the North Atlantic, is of outstanding national and international importance and deserves appropriate international protection;

4. The RMS Titanic represents a special opportunity for scientific exploration of the deep sea.

B) Objectives:

The Congress declares that Sections 450RR through 450RR-6 of this Act serve the following purposes:

1. To support international efforts to designate the wreck of the RMS Titanic as an international maritime memorial to those who lost their lives aboard the ship in 1912;

2. To encourage the United States to enter into negotiations with other interested nations to reach an international agreement to promote the designation of

RMS Titanic as an international maritime memorial,
and to preserve the scientific, cultural and historical
significance of RMS Titanic;

3. To support the development and establishment of
international guidelines for the research and, when
appropriate, recovery of RMS Titanic;

4. To express the opinion of the United States
Congress that until such arrangements or guidelines
are established, no person shall alter, destroy, or
salvage the RMS Titanic while research activities are
already underway.

Sometime later, the now deceased BMW second-hand dealer, George Tulloch, founded his own salvage company, RMS Titanic, Inc., without further ado and then actually secured the salvage rights to the wreck of the TITANIC.

Since it turned out that it was still possible to make a lot of money with the sunken luxury liner, the recovery of artifacts began systematically.

There were also definite attempts to penetrate the ship's holds, which is absolutely not allowed, but where there's no plaintiff, there's no judge...

There are many pictures of the wreck that reinforce the impression that there was massive looting and destruction down there at a depth of 3800 meters, but these pictures are under lock and key. Some of these pictures appeared briefly on the internet but were very quickly "cashed in".

The accusation that the "new pictures" published so far are already much older is unfortunately not entirely absurd.

But no one (except the salvage company, of course) can say exactly how badly damaged the wreck of the luxury liner really is. In principle, there have never been any truly independent expeditions, and if there have been, they seem to have been ordered to keep their mouths shut.

Even the tourists who have dived to the wreck are only given a pre-produced CD on which short sequences can be seen in which the participants themselves can be seen getting on and off the dive boat, but pictures of the dive they have been on are probably not on their CD.

This was the common practice for tourist diving trips to Titanic in the late 1990s and early 2000s. Old pictures of the wreck may well have been used, because most diving tourists don't notice it anyway.

So here, too, the motto is: New pictures of the TITANIC wreck are not to be seen. How is anyone other than the salvage company RMS Titanic, Inc., supposed to know how the shipwreck really is? Unfortunately, it is to be feared that it will not look very good, because only selected material is shown from the expeditions.

After Robert Ballard dived to the TITANIC again in 2004, he wondered aloud about the disappearing crow's nest (at the front of the mast) of the luxury liner. What is strange about this, however, is that there is a press article in which years earlier, Ballard and George Tulloch blamed each other for the mast being rammed by one of the submarines during one of the dives. It was said at the time that "the mast basket then sank through the open cargo hatch into the hold!"

It was interesting, however, that shortly afterwards it was announced that the bell had been "saved" from the mast. Later this was published with the contradiction that the bell had been found in the wreckage. Was one not sure about public opinion regarding the damage to the wreckage? Already when the wreck was officially found in 1985, Ballard's camera sledge hit the wreck considerably several times due to the enormous current at a depth of 3800 meters and almost got stuck there. In the process, the camera sled also collided with the mast basket. However, the mast basket was later visible, albeit only partially, in later TV documentaries. There is therefore much to suggest that the salvage crews are primarily responsible for the disappearance.

In 2010, RMS Titanic, Inc., made another expedition to the wreck and announced in advance that it would then *"make all film and photographic material available to the public."*

So far, so good. But what happened? After just a few days, no more footage could be found on the internet, and everything was kept under lock and key. So much for *"make all film and photo material available to the public"*....

Unfortunately, the public is still at the "mercy" of the salvage company as far as up-to-date pictures of the

TITANIC are concerned. If RMS Titanic, Inc., doesn't want to, then no one really gets to see current pictures of the wreck.

But that can't really be what the inventor had in mind...

Let us now briefly return to the tourist diving trips to the wreck of the luxury liner.

In the anniversary year of the sinking in 2012, the provider of the diving trips, Deep Ocean Expeditions, DOE for short, wanted to cash in once again and had scheduled four expedition dates, each with up to 20 participants. Two of these dates were already fully booked before the very short-term cancellation took place in early summer 2012. In November 2012, the DOE provided an explanation for the cancelled dives:

The political situation in Russia made a new contract for another expedition with the Akademik Keldysh to the wreck of the TITANIC very unlikely! The material as well as the personnel of the Keldysh (made famous by the blockbuster "TITANIC" by James Cameron), is partly so outdated that one has to think about it seriously.

The Akademik Keldysh is now in service for other projects and Dr. Anatoly Sagalevich, the head of the diving capsule program, went into well-deserved retirement.

This was also the end for the Keldysh team, which had worked well together for many years. Thus, the 2005 TITANIC expedition was the last for the Akademik

Keldysh. This was the end for the tourist diving trips to the Titanic until 2021!

Two years earlier, in August 2019, a rather surprising expedition to the TITANIC took place, led by diving expert Victor Vescovo. In a total of five dives, unique images of the ship were taken in 4K resolution. The expedition found out that, among other things, Captain Edward John Smith's bathtub had disappeared from view because the interior's ceiling had collapsed. Also, the deterioration of the wreck was progressing. But these findings were not all that new.

Let us now return to the tourist diving trips to the TITANIC. In 2021, the American company Ocean Gate launched the first tourist diving expedition in many years. However, they did not call the tourists "tourists" but so-called "mission specialists" who, as crew members on board the diving capsule Titan, take on scientific tasks and have no influence on which parts of the TITANIC they get to see or whether they get to see the wreck at all. The "mission specialists" had to pay 150,000 US dollars for this trip. For the year 2022, further diving trips are planned which are to cost the participant, however proud, 250,000 US dollars.

What is interesting is that the participants were allowed to make and publish actual video and photo recordings of the wreck, which was not possible under the direction of RMS Titanic, Inc., as already described.

The results of the expedition in which the "wreck veterans," Paul-Henri Nargeolet and Rory Golden also took part, were mixed:

In the end, ten dives took place during the five missions, six of which reached the wreck of the TITANIC. The bow was explored twice, the stern once, and various locations in the debris field three times, including previously undocumented ones. Some of the "mission specialists" never saw the TITANIC but had to pay full price. However, they will have the opportunity to see the wreck again in 2022 for "only" 52,000 US dollars.

It seems, the touristic diving trips to the TITANIC will be continued.

The Open Letter from Paul-Henri Nargeolet to Robert Ballard

In 2005, the open letter from Paul-Henri Nargeolet, co-leader of several expeditions to the wreck of the TITANIC, to the self-proclaimed discoverer of the wreck, Dr. Robert Ballard, which is printed here in full length, caused a huge furor in the professional world of TITANIC research. And this letter was a real sensation, because it clears up a lot of legends that Robert Ballard himself has created.

Dear Bob,

I just finished re-reading your December 2004 article in National Geographic entitled, "Titanic Revisited," and I've decided enough is enough. For many years, I've read your published accounts, and I've listened to your televised interviews about Titanic, trying hard to ignore your lack of knowledge about the ship and the expeditions that have visited her. But now your article is sullying the memory of the former RMS Titanic, Inc., president, the late George Tulloch, and I simply cannot continue to look the other way. I want to remind you, Bob, that in 1985 when Titanic was discovered, you were a geologist, not an expert on wrecks. You learned about the "wreck world" at the Titanic site; this was your very first wreck experience.

Your expedition co-leader, Jean-Louis Michel, was an engineer, trained to build and test new equipment. He, too, lacked wreck expertise. You studied rocks, and he studied technology, but those qualifications did not make you an overnight wreck expert. Perhaps the greatest illusion you have perpetuated in the media is how Titanic was discovered. Your account is quite selective, Bob. Important facts have been omitted, information the public deserves to know. In 1977, the HMS Hecate, a hydrographic ship of the British Royal Navy that was mapping the "nuclear submarine road," found a "wreck of a big ship in two parts." You had this information prior to your 1985 expedition.

On July 10, 1985, at 1:13 p.m., in the first hours of your expedition on board Le Suroit, the navigation transponders were deployed, and a large echo was seen on the 12 kHz Edo Western echo sounder. This echo looked like a wreck. The information and the "estimated" position were recorded by the navigation officer on duty in the control room and by the officer on watch in Le Suroit's logbook. According to the officer of the ship who was on the bridge, you decided to ignore this information.

This letter starts really fulminant, because here, Paul-Henri Nargeolet admits that the TITANIC was discovered as early as 1977 and not, as the history books say, in 1985 and that Robert Ballard already had the details of HMS Hecate during his expedition, which had discovered a "large shipwreck in two parts". But let´s read on...

A few days later, the second SAR sonar track began. A large "magnetic anomaly" popped up on the Leti magnetometer, independent from the SAR sonar. The anomaly was in the same area as the one that the echo sounder found on July 10. The two Leti engineers operating the magnetometer were positive something big had been found. Once again, you

46

*rejected this essential information. Could it be that you
wanted to orchestrate the discovery so that your new
equipment could be used to find the wreck? Doing so would
have justified the expedition.*

Here, Nargeolet suggests that Dr. Robert Ballard
wanted to be celebrated as "the discoverer of the
TITANIC" and probably did everything possible to
find the sunken luxury liner "in time" when the
Americans are in charge, and he sabotaged the efforts
of his French partners until then...

*As for the big moment you've talked about countless times on
television, the actual discovery of the ship, let me refresh your
memory as to who was awake and who was sound asleep when
Titanic was "found" (for the third time). At 12:48 a.m.,
September 1, 1985, Jean-Louis Michel was on watch in the
control room of the oceanographic vessel Knorr. Just after the
discovery, the entire crew was called into the ARGO central
command. The only crewmember not present was the cook,
who had gone to wake you in your cabin.*

*It cannot be said enough times that Jean-Louis Michel, your
friend, was on duty at the moment of discovery, but you
conveniently forget that fact. The public has been led to
believe that you single-handedly discovered the Titanic. For
the last 19 years, you've done an excellent job of withholding
the fact that your head was on a pillow, eyes closed, dreaming,
perhaps, when the big event happened.*

*Jean-Louis Michel should have been given the bulk of the
credit. They say fact is better than fiction. Perhaps, in your
never-ending quest to capture the public's attention, you
should consider writing a new book reporting the true story of
Titanic's discovery: A cook goes to wake a sleeping geologist*

47

in his bed on a ship. The geologist opens his eyes, hears the news, and a quiet career suddenly takes off, never to be in the shadows again.

This is well known, because Ballard himself admitted in his book "The Discovery of the Titanic". that he had gone to bed when the first boilers of the Titanic were found and that he finally had to be called by the cook, but in fact Ballard has since then acted as the sole discoverer of the wreck, although it is proven that he slept when it was discovered...

My purpose in writing now is to ask you questions about the Titanic wreck and to help you sort through your mix of rumor, hearsay and so-called facts that you've been issuing to the public. I'm shocked over statements you, as a scientist, have made, such as, "I've heard stories about the damage the mini-subs had inflicted when they land or crash on the ship." Hearsay is not a scientific approach, nor should a scientist be presenting conclusions before examining and verifying his information and/or theory. But I suppose with media there with their cameras and their microphones, you had to say something.

However, it should be noted that Paul Henri Nargeolet, as a repeated participant in expeditions to the wreck, would not admit that the wreck was damaged...

How many wrecks did you see before the Titanic? I ask this question because I'm baffled by your comments about the crow's nest, which, you say, "... the French destroyed." You claim the crow's nest was in good condition in 1985 and 1986. But when I look at the pictures from your expeditions of 1985 and 1986, I see the crow's nest smashed against the mast. It is scarcely "in good condition" after a descent of two-and-a half miles and a big crash on the ocean floor, followed by 73 years in the water. My records indicate that this was your first wreck, Bob. Everything must have looked beautiful to you when you first laid eyes on it. I dove on the wreck 30 times, and over a period of 11 years, I was able to observe the evolution of the deterioration, from my first dive in 1987 to my last dive in 1998. During that time span I saw tremendous changes in the crow's nest, the same kind of changes that were affecting many other parts of the bow and the stern sections. In 1993, little pieces of the crow's nest were still on the mast, but a year later, when we went down in hatch number three with the mini-ROV Robin, those particular pieces were gone. I looked for them on the deck, just under the mast, but I found nothing.

The question whether the mini-robot might have been used to search for the diamonds on board the TITANIC, which were strictly denied by the salvage company until a few years ago, is something I'd rather not ask here...

On your recent National Geographic television documentary, you again accused the French of destroying the crow's nest. But what you probably don't know is that the IFREMER team recorded all of its 119 dives on Titanic. There are 800 hours of videotape, documenting our work from our first expedition in 1987 to our final dive in 1998. I watched all 800 hours of the video, several times, and I can certify that the Nautile never touched the crow's nest during any of our 119 dives. In your December 2004 National Geographic article, you describe submersibles on Titanic as... "bulls in a china shop." I know the submersible pilots, the Alvin pilots and the IFREMER pilots. I also did an expedition with the Russian Mirs and even the Japanese Shinkai 6500. They are all good pilots, Bob. They have much more experience than you have diving on wrecks.

Several years ago, in one of your articles you insulted the Alvin pilots. You were in trouble with them for that, and I had a quick talk with you about that at Woods Hole, just after this incident.

You never dove again in the Alvin since this incident. Now you are insulting all pilots who dove on the Titanic. Are you trying to convince people that you are the only one working the correct way on wreck? You are not a submersible or an ROV pilot and you speak in contradictions. You say Titanic is as fragile as china, and yet you seem shocked by the deterioration. I would like to remind you how strong the currents can be on the wreck. For example, in 1986, when you were diving with the submersible Alvin, you were not going to the aft end of the bow section because the current was so strong, coming from the south and pushing Alvin into the boiler room. The current's speed and direction changed even during a single dive. One day in 1996, we saw the Titanic "smoking."

The current was so powerful, it was perpendicular to the wreck. The water was going inside the wreck through the broken port windows on the upper decks and going out with a lot of sediment by the grand staircase, creating this illusion of smoke. How many times did the power of the currents attack the wreck over the past 91 years, and for how many hours? From my 11-year experience diving on Titanic, I can assure you that the ocean floor around that wreck is not a quiet place. Often it is more like a dishwasher. The daily deterioration caused by the current is far more significant than a submersible landing.

It should be noted that the submersibles will certainly cause some additional current when they are operating down there. If you then consider how the TITANIC

50

looked when she was officially discovered after 73 years and in what condition she is now 20 years later after various diving expeditions, it is clear that the dives must have also affected the wreck pretty badly. Furthermore, you can only judge the drift when you are on site with a dive boat, which itself causes quite a bit of drift. The rest of the year you can't judge in principle, because you are not on site, right?

When a submersible lands on the deck of the Titanic, it is not a Boeing 747 landing. It has no speed; it is in neutral buoyancy, using its vertical thrusters to go down slowly, and when its pilots want to stay somewhere, they add weight in its water tank ballast, but no more than 20 or 30 pounds. What damage could a few pounds spread out over 20 square feet (the average surface area of the bottom of a sub) make? Your "famous" holes on the deck are not caused by submersibles. They grow year after year. If you had more experience with wreck deterioration and shipbuilding, you would know the thickness of a ship's hull is not the same as that of a deck (or a crow's nest). The thickness of the steel plate of the hull is 1"; with the rivets in many places the thickness is 2" and in some places with reinforcement plate, it is 3" (Look at the 20-ton "Big Piece" we brought up, and you will learn that). For years little deterioration was visible, but once the holes started, the phenomenon goes faster and faster. You say to the public there is no oxygen at this depth.

That's true, but that doesn't mean there is no natural deterioration. You know that, having dived on hydrothermal sites, and you know the bacteria eating the wreck don't need any oxygen at all. They eat several hundred pounds of steel per day, everywhere on the ship, including the decks and the crow's nest, but they have more of a difficult task on the hull and it will take them more time to make a hole through 1, 2 or 3-inch steel than through 1/4."

Here, one must also take sides with Ballard because he does not deny that there is natural decay. For he writes: " But the TITANIC must not only endure the consequences of human activity. It also suffers from natural decay. Iron-eating bacterial colonies nibble at its hull. Microbiologist Roy Cullimore estimates that the organisms extract at least 45 kilos of iron from the wreck every day").

You know that, but you don't talk about it, perhaps because the biologist who discovered this phenomenon on Titanic is not from your team and you want to ignore it. Many American, British and Canadian scientific and naval engineering experts worked with us on the wreck, and they did a very good scientific job. We were a team; we were not doing a one-man show. You mention the international treaty to protect Titanic as though you originated this idea. With my friend George Tulloch, I was at the first discussion about this international treaty to protect Titanic, but we never saw you there; you appeared 15 years later. The sea is the last free place in the world. I hope the treaty will not mean the end of that. You attacked my best friend, George Tulloch. He said nothing while he was alive, just smiling, but you continued after his death, and I can't let you do that and remain silent. George was working with his heart. He loved Titanic, certainly more than you. He stopped all other activity for his new passion. He came from a different world, the "business world," but you did, also: Geology never helps scientists to better understand "the wreck world." I spoke about that with many geologists, and all told me, "PH, I know nothing about the wreck world." Everyone learns by studying and diving. You started in 1985, not before. I can tell you that as a naval officer, an underwater demolition team captain, a deep diver, an ROV pilot, a submersible pilot and a technical leader or leader of many expeditions on ship sinkings dating from before the time of Christ to today. George Tulloch learned very quickly, more quickly than most people. You probably remember the 1985 contract between Wood Hole Oceanographic Institution (for whom you were working) and IFREMER which said that IFREMER would own the rights to the pictures if the wreck was found. That was because Woods Hole obtained its money for the expedition from the U.S. Navy, and IFREMER had to find the money to finance its expedition. (IFREMER, like WHOI, can't use its own money for this kind of expedition.) When the ship was found, you decided to break the contract. A helicopter flew to the Titanic site on Sunday, September 1, hours after the discovery (how they could come so quickly to the site is another story) and picked the pictures up. You decided to give the pictures to the media, and used them for your own purposes.

In the next few years, you gave a lot of lectures and made a lot of money with these photos. You mention that fact in your last book, but it is very fuzzy, as if it was not your decision. Were you the leader of the expedition, or not?

This dispute has been smoldering since 1985, and it seems that Ballard wanted to distinguish himself as "the discoverer of the TITANIC" at the expense of his French partners, whom he apparently deceived. And indeed, he succeeded, because the history books only identify him as the discoverer and only mention in subordinate clauses that the French were "involved"...

I remember 1986, when we were expecting to do the first French-American Titanic expedition together, using Alvin and Nautile with the two little ROV's, Jason Jr. and Robin.

53

You were expecting to recover artifacts until the U.S. Navy forbade you from recovering anything from the site. The U.S. Navy didn't want to give you any chance to trick IFREMER as you did the year before. You were lucky IFREMER is a government institution and doesn't like trouble. (If you break a contract, as you did in 1985, but with a private company, you could well be sued.)

You always mention the thousand artifacts "from the wreck." It contains over 50,000 artefacts, most of them south or around the stern. It is indeed true that we brought up the bronze mast light in 1987 and published photos of it. It is true we took the bronze mast light in 1987; we published pictures of that. The light was not bolted onto the mast, but like all of them, was held in place by two inserted vertical steel pins, and the video shows we didn't even break the two pins, very fragile, when we removed the light. I remember the light was on the part of the mast lying on the bridge deck and far from the crow's nest. Now it is a beautiful artefact in a public exhibition. The bell was recovered from the debris field close to the stern, half a mile from the crow's nest. Its surface is permanently scarred from lying in the acidic sand (personally, I'm not sure it is the bell from the crow's nest — there were five bells on the Titanic).

The question arises why at exhibitions of the RMS Titanic, Inc., it is still rigidly and firmly claimed that it comes from the crow's nest of the TITANIC. At the exhibition of RMS Titanic, Inc., in Kiel (Germany) in 2007, it was even claimed that this bell had been installed on board the ship in a used condition, as the traces of use inside the bell would indicate that it had been in use for a longer period of time. Furthermore, this would have been common practice at that time to save money. Well, who should believe that...?

Yet you have said that the crow's nest was damaged when we recovered the bell. Upon what evidence do you base this statement? You suggest the Mir broke the bulkhead of Captain Smith's room. That also is not true. Do you have any evidence of that, or is it only hearsay? I asked Anatoly Sagalevitch about that, and he swears the Mir never did it. I trust him. The bulkhead was detached from the roof, and you can see that from your 1985 mosaic and from our 1998 mosaic. (Yes, we did one, a very good one.) The wall fell down more and more year after year. Time, the currents and the bacteria did the job; they don't need any help. Time is the worst enemy of the Titanic. When we dove in 1996 on the Britannic, a sister ship of the Titanic that sank a few years later (on Sunday, 19 November 1916, during the First World War, author's note) in shallow water, we found that the glass dome of the grand staircase is still in place, intact. The entire wreck is in a much better condition, demonstrating that depth doesn't protect the Titanic at all. The bacteria eat the wreck more quickly than any corrosion.

It should be noted that the Britannic was not subjected to the same destructive forces during her sinking as her sister TITANIC, nor did she break in two, nor implode during her sinking like the TITANIC. Therefore, the comparison that Nargeolet draws here is a bit misleading, in my opinion.

No one has landed "with a heavy craft near the entrance of the grand staircase, a popular landing site." The roof was already collapsed in 1985, and you can see that on your 1985 mosaic, too. The roof of the gymnasium collapsed by itself between 1993 and 1994; I have mentioned that to you many times. When a sub lands on a deck, or anywhere, it weighs no more

than 40 pounds because it is ballasted to neutral buoyancy.
Talking about "a bull in a china shop," when you dove in the
Mediterranean with the NR1 — a very heavy U. S. Navy
submersible of more than 350 tons, 20 times heavier than the
Alvin, the Mirs or the Nautile — you brought up amphorae
from antique wrecks, saying to the Italian archaeologists (who
were very angry about your salvaging activities) that the
wrecks are in international waters.

Like the TITANIC, by the way, but this is repeatedly
ignored by the American salvage company, which has
been granted the rights, even though it is a British
ship, which has not even sunk in American waters...

It is interesting that information about this salvaging
disappeared from the "Jason Project" website, and it was after
your first Titanic expedition. The public can see in public
exhibitions the artefacts we brought up and restored. I don't
know what happened with "your" amphorae; I saw only one at
your house behind you during one of your TV interviews, and
there are some at Mystic. You said the Roman and Greek
wrecks are still there after 2,000 years, and so why not the
Titanic?

Are you joking? The only parts of these ancient wrecks visible
are their cargo: amphorae, marble blocks and columns, but
never their wooden hulls. When we find 10 or 20% of a
wooden hull under the sediment, it is a big discovery, but 90%
of the artifacts are invisible. The only way to find them is to
dig. You are full of contradictions. When you were in a
junkyard looking at the Lusitania's propeller, you were sad,
and I am, too. Then you said you would understand and agree
to the propeller's recovery if it was for a museum. Are
Lusitania artifacts good for exhibition, but Titanic's artifacts
are not? Are they not both "historic" wrecks? Do we have to

56

wait 2,000 years before starting to work on "historical" wrecks, when 90% of the information will have disappeared? Is this your "scientific approach" to the problem? Do you think watching live television is enough for the public, who just has to watch you talking while a robot is diving and trust you about what is still on the bottom of the ocean? What do you preserve by doing that? You talk about "such a comedy," but those who know better are not laughing. I never read any expressions of concern from you about the Central America, the Republic, the Monitor or other wrecks. I don't understand the difference between those wrecks and Titanic. Many people lost their lives in these tragedies, too. Is it because you were not involved with these expeditions that they don't exist for you? Are you trying to protect the five million wrecks all around the world, or just "your" wreck?

Since 1986 you have often mentioned the shoes you saw on the bottom, like an obsession. When people travel, they generally have several pairs of shoes in their luggage, and with more than 2,200 people on board, that means many pairs of shoes. In the best ocean liners of 1912, passengers left their shoes in the corridors where the ship's "boots" would polish them overnight. Somehow you are able to describe with detail the supposed position of each body on the bottom, but once again, you fail to mention that when a ship sinks, most people try to escape from it. That means most are outside the ship when it sinks. Some of them may have been trapped, but they are probably still in the wreck, although you admit in one of your books that all human remains had disappeared within five years.

So, as few people as Nargeolet describes here were not inside the TITANIC when she sank. Some experts assume that there were probably nearly 500 passengers inside the sinking ship, which I think is a bit high.

57

If they were not in the ship, they were drifting with the Gulf Stream, almost all of them with life jackets and without their shoes. We know Titanic was in the Gulf Stream on this night, as she was east of her estimated position. A body sinking without a life jacket descends very slowly, drifting very far from the site. The chance for a body to land close to the stern, with legs perfectly parallel, where most of the shoes you mention are located, is infinitesimal, and a mother's shoes close to her long-haired daughter's shoes have no chance to be together. There is a 99% chance the shoes came from a suitcase or from a cargo hold. The sinking of Titanic is dramatic enough without such absurd assertions.

Recently you said you want to paint Titanic's hull. I hope that is a joke. Your proposed project reminds me of the man in the 1950's who wanted to straighten up the "Leaning Tower of Pisa" in Italy with his car and a cable. If you want to preserve the wreck for few more years, you have to paint both sides, not only the exterior as you said. And, of course, before you begin to paint, you will have to brush the hull to remove all the rusticles, and vacuum all the ship to remove the tons of sediment and the "orange spots" on the wreck. These spots are made by the rusticles when they fall down or are blown away by the current, not by the "heavy craft landing or crashing," as you claim. You never went inside the wreck, even with Jason Jr. – you were just at the top of the grand staircase where you took picture of the chandelier.

When we were inside the wreck, we saw the same rusticles made by bacteria inside and outside the ship (Cameron's July 2005 television documentary confirms what I say here). I don't want to talk about the pollution your proposal would cause, with thousands of gallons of paint being dispersed through the water. The tankers you talk about are not painted

58

in open water. The shipyards do that to save money and not strain the ship in a dry dock. Good luck with your "painting project." What are you trying to preserve: the wreck, nature, or your celebrity? Be honest: Do you think the "corrosion" or the bacterial activity protects the ship?

If, in some places, you can see clean metal, that will change; it happens all the time on a wreck. Like all the wrecks in the world, Titanic's condition will become worse and worse, year after year. Nothing will stop time, Bob, not even your brush and pot of paint. You said, "A protocol for visitors should be established." Probably you will volunteer to write it. "It's like you don't go to Gettysburg with a shovel," as you said, or, "These heavy craft are like bulls in a china shop, and Titanic's china is getting broken." Remember, you were playing with the artifacts during your dives in 1986 without any special tools: Shaking the third class safe by its handle in the debris field, and moving a coffee cup from the ocean floor to the top of a boiler for the purpose of taking a "dramatic picture."

The story with the coffee cup is indeed an audacity that Ballard afforded himself, because in his book "The Discovery of the Titanic" he mentions this coffee cup explicitly and also reproduces a photo of it and claims: "A tin cup and a door handle came to rest next to the red firing door of a boiler. At another point we were examining the outside of a boiler; on top of the lid was a rusty metal cup of the kind used by the crew, as if a stoker had put it there before the water had entered the boiler room "

That he placed it there himself is an absolute cheek...

What do you want for Titanic? Do you wish to be the only one diving on the wreck? During the 1986 Titanic expedition, you *were the only passenger in Alvin; you did all the dives and you let no one else dive. Now many people have dived, even "tourists," and it is good. The Titanic site is not private land.*

Strange, then why does the salvage company give this impression?

You are not the only one who respects the wreck. All the divers did. There may be eccentric people who dove, but it is not the end of the world. Funerals and weddings occur in the same edifice, church, mosque, or pagoda. That's what I would say to you if I were one of those spirits who talk to you when you are on the site. Are you a mystic now? Some animation is not bad in the kingdom of the darkness. James Cameron did a very good movie about Titanic, and I'm happy the world loves this movie. Everyone has the right to dream about Titanic, to see the wreck if they want, and to see artifacts. It must not be the privilege of a small group of people.

But what it is de facto, at least as far as diving down to the wreck is concerned...

Your article gives a list of artifacts, trying to make fools of the salvagers. The world's archaeologists are doing the same as we did, taking pictures and video, recovering artifacts, mapping the sites. It is a long job to do that. On a historical wreck it is the same process. We took pictures, mapped the artifacts in the debris field, recovered them (sometimes with a dedicated tool built just for one artifact), brought them up to the surface and then aboard the ship, properly stored them, and carried them to a professional laboratory for conservation before they could be exhibited to the public.

Fifteen million people visited the Titanic exhibitions around the world and enjoyed doing so. These salvage operations are

60

delicate and expensive. You don't know what we did and how we did it. You "heard." And in all the contracts George Tulloch signed with IFREMER for the five expeditions we did, we promised the artefacts could not be sold and would be shown to the public. The Discovery Channel, working with a group of scientists, made a complete study of the wreck and broadcast an excellent series of documentaries about the 1996 and 1998 expeditions.

Unfortunately, and I'm sorry for it, we never published a final report with all the information about our expeditions and their findings. I started such a report, following a meeting with some world-famous archaeologists, who asked me to do it after checking our database. In 1999, a hostile takeover of RMS Titanic, Inc., the salvor-in-possession of the Titanic, stopped this project, but the data, the mosaic, the pictures and the video of 119 Nautile dives in five expeditions conducted by George Tulloch and myself and our team on the Titanic wreck still exist and, I hope, will be available to the public someday. Bob, you are a very good salesman. You sell yourself very well, doing the promotion of your books, doing many lectures and making a lot of money, which is very good for you and makes me happy for you. Why do you have to condemn the jobs done by other teams? Not everyone has the chance to be sponsored by government institutions or funded by taxpayers.

Your expeditions have used U. S. Navy and NOAA equipment. When cruise ships "circled the site," they did so to finance the expedition, not for a show. Elisabeth Navratil, daughter of a survivor, wrote to me a letter saying that her father, Michel, had told her after his trip aboard a cruise ship to the Titanic site in 1996, George Tulloch gave him the best present he ever received in his life, bringing him to the site of the Titanic, where his father died, 84 years after the sinking...

Is this what you call "such a comedy"? I'll stop now, but I can write so much more about all your contradictions, which show your incompetence in dealing with this "world wreck." We are tired of hearing you say, "Let me dive for you and watch what I'm doing." Stop treating your public like idiots. Commander Paul-Henri Nargeolet Expedition Co-Leader, 1987, 1993, 1994, 1996 and 1998 Titanic Research and Recovery Expeditions

After studying this very explosive open letter, the following can be noted:

1. The wreck of the TITANIC was already discovered by HMS Hecate in 1977 and not only in 1985 by Dr. Robert Ballard.

2. Ballard knew the coordinates of the Hecate discovery eight years earlier (and certainly also the details of Jack Grimm's screw blade discovery) and based his later search on them.

3. Ballard seems to have done everything possible to prevent the wreck from being discovered earlier under the leadership of the French.

4. Ballard himself was asleep when the first pieces of wreckage (a boiler) were discovered and Jean-Louis Michel, a Frenchman, was, if you like, the real "discoverer" of the wreck and not Robert Ballard. We leave HMS Hecate out of the picture here.

5. To market his books more effectively, Ballard
    even manipulated recordings on the seabed by,
    among other things, placing a coffee cup on a
    boiler and then pretending that *"a stoker had
    placed it there before the water had entered the boiler
    room."*

Of course, Dr. Robert Ballard did not miss the
opportunity to write a counterstatement. In number 172
of the Titanic Historical Society (THS) journal, he wrote
an 18-page letter in response to Nargeolet's accusations.
Six of these pages were illustrated, and in the text,
Ballard basically only wanted to bring his own ego to the
fore. He said that he, as the scientist, had explored more
wrecks than Nargeolet and that he, as the marine
biologist, also had more knowledge of everything than
Nargeolet. And it went on and on. Very unsatisfactory.

He did not respond to Nargeolet's reproaches once. He
only insisted that he was still the discoverer of the
TITANIC because the expedition was under his
leadership...

This reply letter did more harm than good to Ballard's
already rather tarnished reputation in the TITANIC
world.

The two contenders fought for quite a while until
suddenly a cuddle course was taken. And almost 18
years later, this open letter is nearly forgotten, therefore,
it is all the more important to remember this letter.

A small piece to smile at, at the end of the chapter: At
the TITANIC exhibition in Kiel (Germany) in 2007,

which has already been mentioned here once before,
the scientific advisory board of the exhibition claimed,
by the way, that the organ of the sister ship Britannic,
which had appeared shortly before in Switzerland, but
had not been installed because of the outbreak of war
in 1914, was in any case genuine, because the wrong
spelling "Britannik" would indicate this. The
reasoning must be taken in one's stride, for it reads
something like this: "If it's spelled wrong, it's not a
fake, but if it's spelled right, it's a fake." This is no
joke, by the way. That's what was really claimed. Oh,
my goodness...

The Dispute about the Wreck of the TITANIC

A sad chapter in the history of the TITANIC is without doubt the legal dispute over the salvaged artifacts of the ship that lasted for years and flared up shortly after the official discovery of the wreck at a depth of 3,800 meters.

The questionable fact that an American court felt compelled to award the salvage rights to a (naturally) American company has already been discussed here.

The former used car dealer George Tulloch had at the time rather quickly founded his own salvage company called RMS Titanic, Inc., and had the salvage rights awarded to him (see also chapter "How Much is the Wreck Really Damaged?").

RMS Titanic, Inc., carried out expeditions to the wreck and organized exhibitions such as the famous exhibition in Hamburg (Germany). In 1998, it was taken over by the entertainment company SFX, but kept its old name.

Five years later, things got very turbulent, because on Tuesday, 18th November 2003, a lawsuit was filed against three former directors of the old RMS Titanic, Inc.

At issue were none other than former founder and president George Tulloch, Nautile pilot Paul Henri Nargeolet (already well known to us) and advisor Allan Carlin. The court's accusation was that Tulloch and

Nargeolet, with the knowledge of Allan Carlin, distributed a considerable amount of salvage to friends and relatives and also passed on video material from various diving trips to them.

According to the indictment, the damage amounted to over four million US dollars. George Tulloch then announced that he would *"really spill the beans in court!"* But this never happened because Tulloch died of cancer two months later. The case was later dropped "for lack of evidence".

However, another trial against RMS Titanic, Inc., came to a verdict, as on Tuesday, 26th October 2004, high-ranking executives of the former RMS Titanic, Inc., were fined for making false statements when they took power in 1998 that toppled George Tulloch as president. Since then, the entertainment company SFX was the salvage rights holder and Arnie Geller was installed as president of RMS Titanic, Inc. Others convicted were Michael Harris, John Joslyn, Joseph Marsh, David Lucas, Steven Sybesma, as well as John Thompson and Arnie Geller.

While the trial was still ongoing, RMS Titanic, Inc., was dissolved and reincorporated on Friday, 15th October 2004 as Premier Exhibition, Inc.

The president of Premier Exhibition, Inc. was, believe it or not, Arnie Geller.

In July 2005, the news suddenly broke: RMS Titanic, Inc., is back as a 100% subsidiary of Premier Exhibition, Inc.

Since then, the "former" salvage company has only been responsible for marketing "in-house" exhibitions. The business path is interesting: First, the company against which various lawsuits had been filed a year earlier is deleted or renamed. Since one cannot condemn a company that no longer exists, the name was "bought" and brought back to life under considerable restriction of rights. Premier Exhibition, Inc., no longer had to be accused of "renting out" the exhibits - the "new/old" subsidiary is now there to charge for the items and the subsidiary, then deducts the costs as a tax burden. Perfect!...

In 2006, RMS Titanic, Inc., approached the US Congress saying that the wreck was deteriorating too quickly and that history must now be preserved. But, although everything happened quietly and unnoticed by the public, the salvage company got into trouble because the agreement was again not ratified by the participating countries.

Note: A few years earlier, the old salvage company had already approached the governments in Great Britain, France, and Canada via Congress to initiate an agreement to "protect the wreck." The salvage company wanted an agreement in which they alone would be allowed to decide who could dive to the wreck and what should be done there. It was quickly pointed out how important it was now to be allowed to carry out salvage operations inside the TITANIC.

The USA was to be left in charge of all matters concerning the wreck, and the geographical location of the wreck was to be marked and recorded as the first international maritime memorial. It could be inferred between the lines that no more tourist diving trips should take place.

According to the draft, diving expeditions were to be approved individually, thus reducing the number of dives. This only led to the conclusion that the Americans now only wanted to authorize dives that were in their own interest.

It is therefore not incomprehensible that the other countries did not follow suit...

In May 2007, they went one better by suddenly claiming that illegal dive looting had taken place in the summer of 2005 and the summer of 2006...

But strangely enough, nothing is known about it! In the case of "Operation Bluelight" (an illegal diving trip that took away some of the wreckage), they at least knew about the Northern Horizon, a research vessel that had been booked for three months.

Curious about the RMS Titanic, Inc., claim, however, is that an American/Russian expedition took place in the summer of 2005. Was this expedition illegal?...

In the summer of 2006, all dives were cancelled without any reason being given, so how does RMS Titanic, Inc., suddenly know that considerable damage was caused to the wreck by the plunderers in 2005 and 2006, when they themselves were not on the wreck?

RMS Titanic, Inc., did not remain inactive and even made representations to the British government to plead for all worldwide TITANIC activities to be placed under the management of RMS Titanic, Inc.

Suddenly, the salvage company's makers even referred to Robert Ballard's expedition in 2004 (which eventually led to Paul-Henri Nargeolet's open letter) when he sharply criticized the massive damage to the wreck due to the salvage operations. Piquantly, it was RMS Titanic, Inc., itself that attacked Ballard here....

In 2006, by the way, a court in America ruled in a lengthy trial that RMS Titanic, Inc., was not the owner of the salvaged goods of the TITANIC. According to the court, the company was indeed provided with the salvage rights, but this did not guarantee it ownership. Of course, the salvage company did not let this go and suddenly got support from England, the real home of the TITANIC.

In a supplementary application, RMS Titanic, Inc., was granted confirmation of ownership rights over the future recovered artifacts by the insurance company Liverpool and London Steamship Protection and Idemnity Association, Limited.

Meanwhile, in the USA, Judge Rebecca Beach Smith of the Norfolk District Court had taken up the case. At the time, she could by no means have foreseen that she would have to deal with the TITANIC for so long.

In the summer of 2011, in front of invited guests, she got to see the first images of the wreck, which were taken in a kind of 3D Sonarscan of the ship and the associated debris field. The screening with 3D glasses brought images of unprecedented grandeur of the wreck, as one could also clearly see inside the ship.

In the process, experts from salvage company RMS Titanic, Inc., spoke of how the occasion would also have allowed them to see the long crack in the hull that the iceberg damaged as it tore open the starboard side of the ship.

The president of the parent company Premier Exhibitions, Inc., Chris Davino, also revealed in court the further salvage intentions of RMS Titanic, Inc., by stating that also, *"More and more environmental disasters are threatening the wreck of the TITANIC, and therefore, some things should be saved before it might be too late. But it's too expensive to always have to pay for such expeditions, so we need permission to sell the artefacts freely."*

The judge then wanted to know from Chris Davino when they intended to dive.

"We can't say that for sure yet because of the cost, but maybe next year again!"

Chris Davino went on to state in court that he could well imagine showing the 3D footage shown in court *"to the public one day."*
How nice, the author can only say, or rather write....

On Thursday, 18th August 2011, Beach-Smith handed down a serious verdict with far-reaching consequences for the wreck, the artifacts and the history of the TITANIC.

She awarded the ownership of around 3000 salvaged items from the wreck to the salvage company RMS Titanic, Inc. The judge stipulated that the items may only be sold "as a complete collection" and that the salvage company must ensure that the items are properly handled and stored afterwards.

The question of what happens to the other pieces from the seabed remained unanswered.

In total, more than 5500 items are said to have been recovered, of which about 1800 are stored in France at IFREMER and thus beyond the control of the salvage company. But even otherwise, RMS Titanic, Inc., would hardly reclaim these artifacts, because then the French could really strike out as far as the ownership of the wreck of the TITANIC is concerned...

Since an unknown number of artifacts were already "brought to the people" during the time of the late George Tulloch, there are still far more than the 3,000 artifacts awarded to the salvage company by the court. Not to mention the illegal "Operation Bluelight" which took place at the beginning of the new millennium and from which countless recovered artifacts were hawked to the highest bidders....

For a better understanding: At the end of April 2004, it became known in the US media that there had been a secret mission to the wreck of the luxury liner under the code name "Bluelight" in October 2002. What was initially only a rumor circulating the world was thus confirmed. Interesting is the connection with the indictment that was already staged against Tulloch and Co. in November 2003! Arnie Geller (the then president of the salvage company RMS Titanic, Inc.) denied any knowledge of this "secret operation".

The fact is, however, that the Northern Horizon secretly, quietly left its home port and only returned to Liverpool after two months. On board were the most experienced experts with the most modern equipment to easily access the first class holds. Geller, at any rate, knew nothing after George Tulloch's death. And later, the salvage company even denied its originally expressed intentions to sell over 3,000 salvage artifacts.

Later, more details came to light: The Northern Horizon was chartered for the period from October 2002 to December 2002. The Florida-based company, Ocean Resources, Inc., was responsible for this. Interestingly, however, an unmanned submarine was booked in France, not from IFREMER, but from the company L.D. TRAVOCEAN. The diving trip only took place because RMS Titanic, Inc., wanted to give up the salvage rights, and they would come to an agreement with them, they said... Exciting like a thriller, isn't it?

Not too much time had passed after the court ruling when Premier Exhibitions, Inc., announced at a shareholders' meeting that it wanted to completely restructure itself, as it wanted to go new ways with its subsidiary RMS Titanic, Inc. That this would come about was due not least to the judgement of Rebecca

Beach-Smith. With this judgement, it would now be advisable to reposition the companies.

The majority investor Mark Sellers of Sellers Capital, Inc., explained: *"Also because of the new Titanic euphoria, the top priority now is to increase profits. To do this, another company needs to be set up!"*

Under the new name Premier Exhibition Management (PEM), it will be possible to better market all the companies separately in the future, according to Sellers. In his opinion, it would make sense to found another subsidiary with the new PEM, which could then buy the artifacts from RMS Titanic, Inc., *"since only a complete sale would be possible,"* according to the court order.

Thus, firstly, RMS Titanic, Inc., would have earned its money. And for all further marketing steps, Premier Exhibitions, Inc., or Premier Exhibition Management would operate as the superior body.

"PEM would receive commissions through these services as an intermediary, and one could also earn further profits through future licensing. This would then also apply to all videos, photos and cartography to be marketed further!" explained Sellers. Above all, the current consortium of companies would retain control over the salvage pieces and can continue to rake in the profits on their own...

Shortly afterwards, Mark Sellers first announced internally that a US auction house had already been commissioned to resell the artifacts in 2012 - individually.

In consultation with the client, Guernsey Auctioneers in New York announced that the individual pieces, which were "already part of the first part of the auction," would not be announced until 16th April 2012. A commission percentage of 8% is already expected, which in relation to the expected profit, should mean around five million US dollars in commission alone.

On Thursday, 4th April 2012, shortly before the 100th anniversary of the tragedy, UNESCO placed the wreck of the TITANIC under the protection of its organization as a World Heritage Site.

The Secretary General of UNESCO, Irina Bokova stated in Paris:

"The sinking of the TITANIC is anchored in the memory of humanity. It must therefore not become the target of explorations deemed unscientific or immoral. No wreck has suffered as much from greed as the TITANIC. All these old wrecks are archaeological sites that have scientific value; they are also the memory of human tragedies that must be treated with the respect they deserve."

Irina Bokova then expressed satisfaction that this decision put an end to the dispute over the TITANIC, as it had belonged to a single state anyway, lying in international waters.

It is remarkable that almost 27 years after the "discovery" of the wreck, someone has finally noticed...

However, the question of the artifacts, which also belong under the protection of UNESCO, remains open.

From now on, the 41 signatory states to the UNESCO Convention can both monitor further diving trips and take appropriate measures when it comes to selling the artifacts.

The problem is, however, that Russia, as one of the main divers to the wreck of the TITANIC, is not one of the 41 signatory states and consequently does not feel bound by it...

Another question is: How will UNESCO monitor the whole thing anyway?

It seems to be more of a declaration of intent, because UNESCO can't really enforce the protection of the wreck.

The fact that an author of a book is sometimes overtaken by current events has certainly happened to several other book writers. But what happened after the big-name auction of the TITANIC artifacts surprised even the author:

The auction, which was widely reported worldwide simply did not take place to the extent announced. And it is still not clear who now has the artifacts of the legendary ship in his possession...

The Guernsey auction house refuses to give any information. And that there will be no solution in the dispute about the artifacts for a long time was revealed only a short time later.

An unspecified group of shareholders and partners founded a company that wanted to buy the artifacts for 189 million US dollars and then make them available to the salvage company. The problem with this, however, was that the people who founded this company all came from the circle of the salvage company and the associated parent company.

In principle, this would mean that RMS Titanic, Inc., would sell the artifacts to itself, in order to be able to sell them individually to the highest bidder which would mean a more than blatant violation of the judgement of Rebecca Beach Smith, who had decided that the artifacts should only be sold as a whole collection. A cheap trick!

In the meantime, Beach Smith had already been confronted with accusations from the worldwide TITANIC movement, which made her aware of what was going on behind the scenes at the salvage company. As a result, the judge felt compelled to control the sale of the artifacts and summoned the parent company, which had made it all up so nicely, back to court for Thursday, 29th November 2012 to have the facts of the new subsidiary explained in more detail.

This caused the share price of Premier Exhibition, Inc., which had been soaring in the meantime, to plummet.

Confronted with all these things, Smith decided to take another close look at the case of the TITANIC artifacts, and the thriller about the artifacts continued unexpectedly because in May 2015, the company opened an exhibition building on Fifth Avenue in New York City where the two exhibitions "Saturday Night Live:

The Exhibition" and "The Discovery of King Tut" took place. However, that turned into a huge flop, and on June 14th, 2016, Premier Exhibition, Inc., had to file for bankruptcy.

Before the insolvency court, Premier Exhibition, Inc., wanted to maintain that a part of the TITANIC collection could be sold to pay off the debts. But that contradicted the rulings that had been made up to that point, because RMS Titanic, Inc., was granted ownership rights only on the condition that the collection be kept together as a whole and not sold to private parties.

In court, Premier Exhibition, Inc., argued that they only wanted to sell a small fraction of the collection and that 95.5% would remain together.

Premier Exhibition, Inc., stated in August 2016 that it could, "Without any problems," sell part of the so-called "French TITANIC artifacts." France has no claim or interest in the TITANIC items, Premier Exhibition, Inc., claimed in court. The U.S. State Department, however, contradicted this claim and referred "for the protection of France" to the agreements in force between RMS Titanic, Inc., and France, according to which the renunciation of the artifacts is only valid on condition that they are used "purely culturally" in perpetuity.

That is, they may be displayed in exhibitions but not sold. The judge then followed the argumentation of the Ministry of Foreign Affairs and strictly rejected a partial sale of the "French artifacts" to private buyers. Subsequently, however, Premier Exhibition, Inc., sought to have the courts in France determine that France had no claim to the collection and therefore could not be cited in bankruptcy court as an argument to prohibit the sale of a portion of the "French" artifacts" for budgetary reorganization. Premier Exhibition contacted the French Embassy in the U.S. and set a deadline within which France could assert any ownership claims. However, there was no response from France, and so in August 2017, the bankruptcy court ruled that the "French" artifacts" now also belong to Premier Exhibition, Inc./RMS Titanic, Inc.

In the fall of 2018, the 5,500 artifacts from the TITANIC were all for sale after the bankruptcy filing of Premier Exhibitions in the United States. The National Maritime Museum, National Museums Northern Ireland, Titanic Belfast, and Titanic Foundation, Limited, had joined together as a consortium that raised money to purchase the artifacts. They intended to keep all the items together as a single exhibit. The museums were critical of the bid process set by the bankruptcy court which set the minimum bid at 21.5 million US dollars (£16.5m). The consortium did not have enough funding to meet that amount and was unable to place a bid on the specified date, 11th October 2018.

On 18 October 2018, the relevant court announced that the artefacts may be sold for 19.5 million US dollars to the Hong Kong-based hedge fund consortium, which includes Apollo Global Management, Alta Fundamental Advisors and PacBridge Capital Partners (HK) Ltd. This was a low blow for all those interested in TITANIC...

A critical opinion piece published in June 2020 accused Premier Exhibitions and specifically its subsidiary R.M.S.

Titanic, Inc, of foul play over the auction of the artifacts, suggesting they declared bankruptcy to get around its commitment to keep the collections together and on public display. The piece described the company as "bandits" and "not fit for purpose."

A further controversy arose in 2020, when RMS Titanic, Inc., announced plans to retrieve TITANIC`S wireless radio and exhibit it. The U.S. government challenged the plan in a filing with the 4th U.S. Circuit Court of Appeals in June, contending that any such expedition, which might "physically alter or disturb" the deteriorating wreck, requires authorization from the U.S. Department of Commerce and would breach an agreement with the U.K. that regulates entry into the hull.

After it became clear that a diving expedition to recover the Marconi Room would probably fail due to a veto by the courts, RMS Titanic, Inc., announced that the plans for recovery had fallen through. The reasons given were that they would not be able to dive because of the Corona pandemic and that the costs of salvage would be disproportionate to the returns, and they would therefore refrain from doing so.

It remains to be seen whether the plans to salvage the Marconi Room have really come to nothing. For many critics, they only served as a pretext to create a so-called "precedent" so that, contrary to previous legal rulings, it would be possible to penetrate the wreck and recover artefacts from there.

To be continued…

A Look into the Future – TITANIC II?

I thought for a long time about to delete this chapter of the book, but I finally decided to let it in the book.

At the height of the TITANIC hype which arose in the context of James Cameron's movie in 1997, some rich people had the idea that it might be possible to rebuild the TITANIC (with the latest safety technology, of course) and send her on her maiden voyage in April 2002, on the 90th anniversary of the sinking of the original TITANIC. First plans of a shipyard in Durban (South Africa) had already become concrete, but those plans by Sarel Gous and his RMS Titanic Shipping Holdings ultimately flopped, and no one heard anything more about them after that.

All of the projects had proved to be too costly and not economically viable, and so they were finally buried by their proponents.

Australian Clive Palmer, however, did not care about these failures and so on Monday, 30th April 2012, he went before the assembled press with his plans for a "TITANIC II" and presented his project:

- Palmer plans to build a fleet of luxury ships, including a "TITANIC of the 21st century."

- The shipping company is to be the Blue Star Line, newly founded by Clive Palmer.

- The ship is to be built at a Chinese shipyard (CSJ Jinling Shipping) with which preliminary contracts have already been signed.

- The differences to the real TITANIC are in the technology and the construction of the ship - instead of the former riveting, this time it will be welded, but that is no real surprise...

- Steve Hall and Daniel Klistorner, two excellent experts on the original TITANIC, have been engaged as project consultants.

- The Finnish company Deltamarin is to accompany the project and ensure that the TITANIC II complies with the current safety and building regulations.

- From D-Deck upwards, the stairwells, cabins and public areas are to be placed according to the model of the TITANIC, with an additional deck between C- and D-Deck - the so-called safety deck with lifeboats that comply with modern regulations.

- An advisory board consisting of descendants of crew members and passengers of the TITANIC will accompany the project.

- The maiden voyage of the TITANIC II is planned for the end of 2016 on the Southampton – New York route (an escort will be provided by the Chinese Navy).

- The length of the TITANIC II is 269 meters. It has nine decks with a total of 840 cabins. Also, restaurants, swimming pools, fitness room, library and much more.

- Cost of the mega-project: Unknown...

- The TITANIC II will be eight centimeters longer than the original, as a camera will be installed at the bow to give visitors the opportunity to be photographed in the Jack and Rose pose...

- On board, it is to remain technology-free as far as possible. For passengers, for example, there is to be no internet.

The TITANIC II in dates:

Total length: 269 m
Broad: 32.2 m
Draught: 7.5 m
GRT: 55 800
Cruising speed: 23 knots
Screws: Three four-bladed screws, each on Azipod propeller nacelles
Lifeboat capacity: 2700 plus 800 places in rafts, etc.
Engine power: 48,000 KW
Bow thrusters: Two per side
Crew: f900

Passengers: f2,435
Cabins: f835
1st class cabins: f372
2nd class cabins: f206
3rd class cabins: f257
Decks: Boat Deck
                    Promenade Deck/A
                    Bridge Deck/B
                    Shelter Deck/C
                    Safety Deck
                    Saloon Deck/D
                    Upper Deck/E
                    Middle Deck/F
                    Lower Deck/G
                    Tanktop

Newly created facilities:

- Theatre with 400 seats
- Casino
- Shopping Mall
- Business Centre
- hospital
- Helipad on the aft deck
- Air conditioning

Facilities inherited from the TITANIC:

- First class: gymnasium, Turkish bath, squash room, swimming pool, grand staircase, smoking salon, veranda and palm garden, Café Parisien, a

la carte restaurant, lounge, dining room, reception hall
- two suites with two bedrooms, a private bathroom, living room with fireplace and private promenade
- Second and third class should be identical wherever practicable
- Radio room
- Captain's quarters with living room and bedroom

From Monday, 9th September to Thursday, 12th September 2013, tests with a model of the TITANIC II took place at the Hamburg Shipbuilding Research Institute (HSVA).

During this test, a 9.3-meter-long wooden model of the TITANIC II was subjected to speed and resistance tests. The behavior of the ship, which was a prototype, was subjected to speeds of 18 to 24 knots. These tests were reportedly successful.

Shortly afterwards, the start of construction was announced as March 2014. Then, in May 2014, Clive Palmer announced at a press conference in Shanghai that the maiden voyage of the TITANIC II would be delayed by two years. The date for the maiden voyage would then be 2018.

To date (as of 2022), construction of the ship has still not begun and it will probably never begin. The TITANIC II project must be considered a failure, like its predecessors at the end of the 90s...

TITANIC Movies

Since the tragic sinking of the TITANIC on 15th April 1912, many movies have been made about the famous ship, and I would like to introduce the most famous film versions on the following pages.

Saved from the Titanic (1912)

Just one month after the terrible tragedy, the newsreel film, "Saved from the Titanic," starring the surviving actress Dorothy Gibson, was released. She wore the same dress she had worn on the night of the disaster in this film, which unfortunately is said to have been lost in a fire at the film company in 1914, which was probably intended to add to the authenticity of the film, as were the images of the Olympic and the Lusitania used in this film.

The making of this film was understandably very upsetting for Dorothy, as re-enacting her own role in the whole terrible event was really beyond her strength.

Director: Etienne Arnaud
Length: 10 min
Cast: Dorothy Gibson, Alec B. Francis, Julia Stuart, John G. Adolfi

In Nacht und Eis (1912)

The German silent film about the TITANIC was made in 1912 under the direction of the Romanian Mime Misu and was considered lost for many years before it resurfaced in Berlin in 1998, when James Cameron's world success "TITANIC" was already enjoying its first great successes in the cinemas.

The film was made "according to authentic reports" about the disaster and was shot on the Baltic coast as well as at the Greipelsee near Königswusterhausen near Berlin, where the model of the TITANIC, carried by empty beer barrels, went down spewing steam, and the captain died a hero's death. Unfortunately, you can see from Captain Smith's face that the water was actually only waist deep.

Director: Mime Misu
Length: 41 minutes (color restored version)
Cast: Waldemar Hecker, Otto Rippert, Ernst Rückert, Willy Hameister

Atlantic (1929)

The sinking of the TITANIC serves as a foil for the plot of the first pure German sound film; a disaster drama outdated in its sensational scenes and its played-out pathos.

Director: E.A. Dupont
Length: 90 minutes
Cast: Fritz Kortner, Elsa Wagner, Heinrich Schroth, Julia Serda, Elfriede Borodin

Titanic (1943)

This Nazi-produced film created myths, especially in Germany, some of which have persisted to this day among the older population, such as the claim that the TITANIC had sailed to her doom out of a desire to break records in the battle for the so-called "Blue Ribbon". It has been proven that the TITANIC could never have achieved this record held by the Mauretania, as she was not designed to do so. The White Star Line was also not threatened with bankruptcy and therefore did not increase its speed to drive up its share price.

The actual director of the film, Herbert Selpin, was arrested during the filming because of negative comments about the Wehrmacht, and "according to the ministry" was found dead in his cell on 1st August 1942. Whether it was suicide or murder remains unclear.

By the time the film was completed in 1943, the war situation had developed so unfavourably for the German Reich that Propaganda Minister Joseph Goebbels feared defeatist repercussions for Germany and did not release the film for German cinemas. The film was only shown in German-occupied foreign countries, as a shipwreck could all too easily have been associated with the fall of the German Reich by German film viewers.

The scenes in the film which take place on the night of the sinking and show the Boat Deck of the TITANIC were shot on board the Cap Arcona, a German ship that was hit by Allied bombers in the Bay of Lübeck (Germany) in 1945, killing several thousand deported concentration camp prisoners.

Director: Walter Klingler, Herbert Selpin
Length: 85 minutes
Cast: Sybille Schmitz, Hans Nielsen, Ernst Fritz Fürbringer, Karl Schönböck

Sinking of the Titanic (1953)

This film tells of the sinking of the TITANIC, but it focuses on the marital problems of the fictional Sturges family.

In the plot of the movie, Julia Sturges, whose marriage has not been right for a long time, wants to leave her husband Richard. She therefore goes aboard the TITANIC with her daughter Annette and her son Norman. Her husband Richard, however, follows her and finally gets a ticket for the maiden voyage of the TITANIC from an emigrant family. Despite their attempts to play down their marital problems in front of the children, the situation escalates more and more. During the voyage, Annette falls in love with Gifford Rogers, who comes from a poor background and courts her, while Richard learns that Norman is not his biological son and comes from an extramarital affair with his wife Julia.

As a result, he feels his honor has been violated and makes the unsuspecting Norman feel it. When the TITANIC hits the iceberg and sinks, Julia, Annette and Norman manage to get a place in the lifeboat, while Richard, like all the men, has to stay on board and wait for his imminent end.

Out of love for his supposed father, Norman gives his place in the lifeboat to a woman and, unnoticed by his mother, leaves the lifeboat to go down with his father "like a man."

A very good film overall, but with some very serious mistakes, such as the TITANIC ramming the iceberg on the wrong side in the film. The fact that the ship is supposed to have sunk at 0.20 a.m. is also quite a mistake.

The film received an Oscar nomination in 1954 in the category "Best Production Design" and was finally awarded an Oscar for "Best Screenplay".

Director: Jean Negulesco
Length: 100 minutes
Cast: Clifton Webb, Barbara Stanwyck, Robert Wagner

A night to remember (1958)

This film was directed by Roy Ward Baker based on the novel of the same name by Walter Lord and was made in England and Scotland.

Advisors to the film were 64 survivors of the TITANIC disaster who were still alive at the time (including the Fifth Officer of the TITANIC, Joseph Boxhall) and whose fate was processed in the film.

Incidentally, the story of the sinking of the TITANIC was told in this film from the point of view of the surviving Second Officer Charles Herbert Lightoller.

As an aside, it is interesting to note that the actor Bernard Fox, who played the lookout Frederick Fleet in this movie, also played in the most famous TITANIC film adaptation of all time by James Cameron almost 40 years later, where he embodied the passenger Archibald Gracie.

This impressive film about the sinking of the TITANIC, which James Cameron later described as a model, won a Golden Globe for "Best Film Drama" in 1959.

Director: Roy Ward Baker
Length: 121 minutes
Cast: Kenneth Moore, David McCallum, Laurence Naismith, Richard Leech, Michael Goodliife, Bernard Fox

SOS TITANIC (1979)

This British-US film by director William Hale was produced with British money and many British actors at the Shepperton Studios in London.

To show the drama of all three classes on the TITANIC, three plots are told in parallel. In first class it is John Jacob Astor who travels to New York with his young and pregnant wife Madeleine. In second class it is the university lecturer Lawrence Beesley who begins a romance with his professional colleague Leigh Goodwin, and in third class the Irish immigrant Martin Gallagher falls in love with an unknown Irish beauty.

This TITANIC adaptation is considered to be technically less successful and confines itself more to the historical facts than to the authenticity of the film set. The TITANIC has not been reconstructed realistically or in scale or appearance in this movie. The furnishings of the sets used for the interior shots were largely in the style of the 1930s.

Some exterior shots reveal that the film was partly shot on the Cunard Line's Queen Mary, for at one point the conning bridge's helm can be seen very clearly, which on the Queen Mary is supported on its own turret.

Furthermore, some shots of the sinking ship resemble comparable sequences from the 1958 film, "A night to remember", which were obviously colorized for this film.

Another parallel to the film "A night to remember" is that the actor David Warner, who plays the schoolteacher Lawrence Beesley in this flick, also appeared 18 years later in James Cameron's Titanic film, playing the valet Spicer Lovejoy.

In 1980, the film received an Emmy nomination in the category "Best Editing."

Director: William Hale
Length: 102 minutes
Cast: David Janssen, Cloris Leachman, Susan Saint James, David Warner

The Titanic (1996)

This TV two-parter was produced in 1996, just one year before James Cameron's world success "TITANIC" was released.

The film is based on the novel "TITANIC: An Illustrated History" and tries to reproduce the historical drama as authentically as possible despite the fiction.

Director Robert Lieberman had parts of the deck of the TITANIC recreated but was not nearly as faithful to detail as James Cameron later was. An entire floor of the ship is missing so that there is only a landing between the Boat Deck and the stern. The shots of the ship from the long shot were made on the computer and therefore look very artificial. Nevertheless, the effort is quite considerable for a television production.

On the whole, the film does not quite live up to the promise of the quite prominent cast. Some historical errors also crept in. For example, it is widely pointed out that the TITANIC did not fire any red flares and therefore, from the Californian point of view, they were not distress flares. This is definitely wrong, because the regulation with the red emergency flares only came after the sinking of the TITANIC.

Furthermore, the designer Thomas Andrews is missing in this film, and Captain Smith blames his First Officer Murdoch for wanting to sail sideways past the iceberg. That this maneuver was the ship's undoing did not come out until much later.

Director: Robert Lieberman
Length: 180 minutes
Cast: Catherina Zeta-Jones, Peter Gallagher, George C.
Scott, Tim Curry

Titanic (1997)

The last and by far the most successful movie about the
sinking of the TITANIC was directed by James Cameron
and retells the story of the maiden voyage of the ship in
April 1912.

A love story with fictional characters (Jack and Rose)
was woven into the facts of the sinking. The film, which
was nominated for an incredible 14 Oscars and won
eleven of them (including the Oscar for "Best Picture"),
had 130.9 million cinema-goers in the USA alone. In
Germany, too, 18 million people saw the film.

Among other things, the film showed never-before-seen
interior shots of the wreck of the TITANIC, to which
Cameron dived down several times. Furthermore, the
TITANIC was recreated in almost her original size,
absolutely true to detail. The interior and exterior of the
film set was modelled exactly on the TITANIC. The
sinking of the ship was also filmed true to the original
with the model. The breaking apart of the TITANIC
during the sinking was also shown for the first time.

This film featured David Warner and Bernard Fox, two actors who had already worked on other TITANIC adaptations:

Bernard Fox – A night to remember (1958)
David Warner - SOS TITANIC (1979)

Director: James Cameron
Length: 189 minutes
Cast: Leonardo DiCaprio, Kate Winslet, Bernard Hill, Victor Garber, Billy Zane, Kathy Bates, David Warner, Bernard Fox, Gloria Stuart, Bill Paxton, Frances Fisher

Closing Words

The sinking of the TITANIC on 15th April 1912 in the icy North Atlantic marked a turning point in the history of seafaring.

What remains, nearly 110 years after the sinking of the TITANIC?

A ship described as "unsinkable" sets off on its first voyage and collides with an iceberg after four days at sea and sinks in two hours and 40 minutes. Due to completely outdated regulations, there are far too few lifeboats on board the ship and even these are not nearly fully manned. More than 1500 people do not survive this freezing night in the North Atlantic.

This heralded the end of an era that would shape shipping even to this day.

Never again was a ship described as "unsinkable" as the TITANIC was over 100 years ago.

Unfortunately, for the more than 1500 people who lost their lives on that terrible night in 1912, this realization came too late.

It was only after the disaster that the regulations for seafaring were changed, such as the number of lifeboats onboard a ship. On the TITANIC, lifeboats were only available for about one third of the total number of people allowed on board.

Since the TITANIC was far from fully booked, in retrospect, one can speak of luck that the maiden voyage of the luxury liner was not fully occupied.

An international ice patrol was set up to report immediately if icebergs appeared on ship routes.

In any case, seafaring became a lot safer after the TITANIC disaster, even though shipwrecks can of course happen from time to time.

One only has to think of the ferry Estonia, which sank on Wednesday, 28th September 1994, killing 852 people. This shipwreck is certainly the most formative of my generation.

I do not want to give the impression that the TITANIC was an "unsafe ship". She certainly wasn't, but so many unfortunate circumstances converged that night that it unfortunately became the most famous ship of all time due to her tragic sinking

After the catastrophe, the TITANIC remained quiet for many decades, and treasure hunters racked their brains for decades about how to find and salvage the TITANIC.

When the wreck was "officially found" on 1st September 1985, the legendary luxury liner came back into people's consciousness.

It was not until James Cameron's blockbuster "TITANIC", which won eleven Oscars, that the hype about the famous ship began.

Unfortunately, this hype has not necessarily been conducive to the history of the ship, because many contemporaries have more and more difficulty distinguishing reality from fiction.

If some interested people have to be told explicitly that the TITANIC really existed and the film depicted the tragedy that actually took place, then that says a lot.

And of course, the salvage company RMS Titanic, Inc., knows how to profit from the sunken TITANIC and the hype surrounding the ship.

Since the salvaged artifacts of the ship can be used to make real money, the preservation of the history has been lost.

The history has been systematically rewritten, partly to justify wreck salvage and partly to avoid admitting things that might be unpleasant for the salvage company. In many cases, no one knows anymore what is truth and what is fiction...

A good example of this is that many statements by survivors were adapted to the new findings after the "discovery" of the wreck.

The survivor Eva Hart, for example, had given an interview to the Texan oil millionaire Jack Grimm for his book "Search for the Titanic" in 1982, three years before the official discovery of the wreck, in the course of which Eva Hart was also asked about the possible break-up of the TITANIC:

Jack Grimm: " *When the ship sank below the surface, some reports indicate that it may have split in half and a bow or some part of the ship came up to the surface before it sank again. Do you have any recollection of it sinking?"*

Eva Hart: "*I saw it sink, and I was screaming with fright. But my mother, who was a very calm person, despite the fact that she had this premonition, swore to her dying day that the ship was in half."*

Jack Grimm: "*Yes, we have had many reports of that effect.*"

Eva Hart: "*She said so. I mustn't say I think it did because I don't know. I think I was too terrified."*

A few years and expeditions to the wreck later, it sounded quite different:

"*I can still see exactly how the ship sank, and the memories of it are the worst for me. I saw the horror with my own eyes, and from that night to this day, I can't help thinking that the ship broke in half while it was sinking. I can still see it in my mind's eye. It was so terrible. I couldn't look away. The front part went down first, and the stern of the ship was sticking out of the water for quite a long time."*

That is more than contradictory then. And there are several other examples where survivors suddenly changed their minds completely...

It seems that the impression had to be created that the British and the White Star Line did not want to admit that the TITANIC broke in two. I would say that was achieved.

Most people have already adopted this view one-to-one and are always very surprised when these contradictions are presented to them. Therefore, it is all the more important to keep the history true so that it is no longer possible to rewrite history in a way that suits one's needs.

We can only hope that enough comrades-in-arms will be found for this task.

For some time now, a new phenomenon has been observed in this context: Some "experts" are now claiming, sometimes vehemently and super-teachingly, that those passengers who said that the ship sank in one piece and also made this known in books and documentaries were forced to say so. It's very interesting how they try to turn the tables. But when it comes to TITANIC, nothing really surprises me anymore...

I have been researching the history of TITANIC since 1985, with a longer break. I have heard and read a lot since then and have met some interesting people. What I have noticed over the years is that many of those who deal with TITANIC and her sad history have absolutely nothing in common with each other.

With some, one can almost speak of enmity. How often I would have liked to shake some of these disputants and remind them that we in the so-called "TITANIC community" are all interested in the same subject. So why so much bad blood? I still don't understand that.

Nobody knows everything or can really know everything about TITANIC. But some people act as if they had eaten the TITANIC wisdom with spoons and were omniscient, almost as if the history of the TITANIC belonged to them alone. Every single person researching the history of the TITANIC has their area that fascinates and moves them the most. No one "owns" the TITANIC alone. She "belongs" to all of us.

I know that I will also cause offence with this book, and many will pick on me because I do not represent the mainstream opinion on TITANIC in some things. But after so many years spent researching the history of TITANIC, I take the right to question critically and to point out some very clear inconsistencies.

Not everything that is spread about the history of TITANIC has to be accepted uncritically without questioning. But many would-be experts, of whom one has never heard before, do so and denigrate those who do not. They are then either "conspiracy theorists" or "very bad book authors." Or simply "idiots."

What can probably never be stopped is that newer and newer legends are formed about the TITANIC. It is no legend that the White Star Line belonged to the IMM (International Mercantile Marine) of the American financier J. P. Morgan. However, this fact does not make the famous luxury liner an American ship, as I have already had to read in some publications.

For example, no one would call the English football record champion Manchester United an American football club just because a major American investor has invested in it. But with the TITANIC, that is exactly what is done. If you then point this out, some "experts" will immediately put you down.

Well, what else can one say?...

For me, the history of this great ship, which unfortunately had such a short lifespan, will always remain fascinating. And I think many others feel the same way.

We can only hope that she will be spared a "second demise."

Norbert Zimmermann, July 2022

Thanks

My thanks go to Anka Schlayer from Titanic Connections for her initial proofreading and her great patience in reading that book. She was a great help with some changes in this book.

Many thanks to my proofreader Julie Hanna. She was a great help to realize this English version of my book.

Last but not least, I thank my friends who have put up with my love for this great ship all these years.

Norbert Zimmermann is a German author and historian and has been researching the history of the TITANIC for almost three decades and has earned a very good reputation as a Titanic historian and has been invited to several Titanic events in English-speaking countries as an author and historian.

Sources

Newsticker of the Titanic-Museum-Germany

National Geographic issue December 2004

The Discovery of the TITANIC - Robert Ballard, 1987

Titanic- Das Ende einer Illusion - Norbert Zimmermann, Books on Demand, 2011

Beyond Reach- The Search for the Titanic - William Hoffmann & Jack Grimm, 1982

Titanic Post No. 82 (December 2012)

The last secrets of the "TITANIC " - Donald Lynch, Ken Marshall 2003

The Titanic in Detail - Tom McCluskie (Bechtermünz Verlag,1998)

A ship accused- Senan Molony (Books on Demand, 2002)

TITANIC- The final words - TV- documentary by James Cameron, 2012

Photo Credits

Titanic Engineers Memorial in Southampton: private photo of the author

Titanic at the docks of Southampton: public domain

Titanic leaving Southampton: collection of the author

The gravestone of Sidney Leslie Goodwin: private photo of the author

The image of the bow of the TITANIC is in the public domain because it contains material created by an employee of the National Oceanic and Atmospheric Administration in the course of his official work.

Titanic societies and websites

Deutscher Titanic-Verein von 1997 e.V

https://www.titanicverein.de

British Titanic Society

https://www.britishtitanicsociety.com

Belfast Titanic Society

http://www.belfast-titanic.com

Titanic Verein Schweiz

https://titanicverein.ch

Titanic Historical Society

https://titanichistoricalsociety.org

Recommended Literature on the Subject:

Walter Lord
A Night to Remember
ISBN: 978-0-553-27827-9

David Haisman
"I'll see you in New York"
ISBN 0-6463-3236-8

David Haisman
Raised on the Titanic – An Autobiography
ISBN 0- 646-33265-1

David Haisman
TITANIC – The Edith Brown Story
ISBN: 978-1-4389-6182-8

Donald Lynch, Ken Marshall
Ghosts of the Abyss
ISBN: 0-306-81223-1

Susan Wels
Titanic: Legacy of the World`s Greatest Ocean Liner
ISBN: 978-0-7835-5261-3

James Cameron
Mission TITANIC
ISBN: 978-3667102393

Malte Fiebing
TITANIC (1943): Nazi Germany's version of the disaster
ISBN: 978-3844815122

Lawrence Beesley
The Loss of The SS Titanic

Simon Medhurst
TITANIC Day by Day (366 Days with the TITANIC)
ISBN: 978 139901 143 3

More books by the author:

Titanic – Das Ende einer Illusion

The legendary luxury liner RMS TITANIC sank in the icy North Atlantic on 15th April 1912 at 2.20 a.m., killing over 1500 people. This book tells the complete story of the TITANIC, starting with her construction, her maiden voyage with the fateful collision with the iceberg and ending with the discovery of the wreck at a depth of almost 4,000 meters.

ISBN 978-3-8423-5034-2, 252 Pages

Schicksal Titanic

The sinking of the TITANIC was a severe trauma for the survivors of the tragedy. This book tells the stories of the survivors and shows, how one of the greatest shipwrecks of all times was experienced by the victims themselves.

ISBN 978-3-8482-2125-7, 184 Pages

TITANIC – Chronology of a Disaster

This book tells the story of the TITANIC from its
planning and finishing in Belfast, Ireland, to her
departure from Southampton. The author of the book
also explains the inconsistencies surrounding the
collision of the TITANIC with the iceberg and describes
what, according to the latest TITANIC research,
happened in the last hours before the sinking. The many
tragic fates of the tragedy are also dealt with in detail, as
well as the later scapegoats of the disaster.

ISBN: 978-3753406473, 370 Pages